Drawing Together to
Develop Self-Control

Drawing Together to
Develop Self-Control

Written by Marge Eaton Heegaard

To be illustrated by children
to help families communicate and learn together

Library of Congress Cataloging-in-Publication Data

Heegaard, Marge Eaton.
    Drawing together to develop self-control / written by Marge Eaton Heegaard.
        p.   cm.
    ISBN 1-57749-101-7 (pbk. : alk. paper)
    1. Self-control in children--Problems, exercises, etc. 2. Art therapy for children.
    I. Title.

BF723.S25 H44 2001
155.4'1825--dc21   00-069175

First Printing: May 2001

Printed in the United States of America
05   04   03   02   01   7   6   5   4   3   2   1

Cover: Cover design by Laurie Ingram Duren
Interior: Spring Type and Design

Publisher's Note: Fairview Press publications do not necessarily reflect the philosophy of Fairview Health Services. For a free current catalog of Fairview Press titles, please call toll free 1-800-544-8207. Or visit our Web site at www.fairviewpress.org.

About this book

This book is designed for children, ages five through twelve, to illustrate with pictures they choose to draw. Younger children may need help understanding some of the words and concepts in the book, but do not offer too many suggestions. This is their book; let them make their own decisions.

I recommend that a child be given a small box of new crayons to illustrate the book. While many children enjoy drawing with markers, crayons often encourage greater self-expression. Older children may prefer to use colored pencils.

Younger children like to illustrate books because images come more naturally to them than words. Older children are more comfortable expressing themselves verbally and may use words with their illustrations.

As you and the child work through the book together, focus on ideas and expression rather than artistic technique. Do not try to protect the child from difficult feelings. As children learn to understand and express their feelings, they develop coping skills that will help them the rest of their lives. If a drawing reveals that the child has misperceived something, correct the misperception gently, if at all. Remember that what a child perceives to be real is as powerful to that child as any reality.

To encourage conversation, periodically invite the child to tell you more about his or her drawings. At the end of each section, you may want to tell the child something you have learned and ask the child to tell you something he or she has learned. When the book is completed, encourage the child to share his or her work with another adult for review and continued learning. Save the book as a keepsake of childhood memories.

Adults can help children develop self-control

Label and accept children's feelings in a neutral way and help them learn to distinguish the difference between feelings and actions.

Do not protect children from difficult feelings. Help them to understand and express feelings in acceptable ways so they will develop coping skills for difficult times of life.

Recognize the early signs of loss of control and suggest a time-out to regain control.

Recognize and avoid power struggles.

Criticize only the behavior, never the person.

Parents must always present a united front in matters of discipline.

Encourage the child to postpone gratification in order to reach a specific behavioral goal.

Be consistent with the child and maintain a positive and respectful attitude.

Do not keep doing things for children that they can do for themselves.

Give children age-appropriate chores to teach responsibility, self-discipline, time management, and self-worth.

Meet all the child's needs, but not all of his or her wants.

This book was designed to use the art process to help children express their feelings and understand basic concepts about behavior. As children develop coping skills, misconceptions may be revealed, conflicts resolved, and self-esteem increased. The book can be used individually or with a group facilitated by a supportive adult who is educated to accept feelings and encourage communication. Typically, a child should complete four or five pages a session, but individual needs may vary.

The text is intended to help children:

To children

This is your book. You will make it different from all other books by drawing your own thoughts and feelings. You do not need any special skills to illustrate the pages. Just use lines, shapes, and colors to draw the pictures that come into your head as you read the words on each page. Have fun.

Begin with the first page and do the pages in order. Ask an adult for help with words or pages you do not understand. When you have done a few pages, stop and share your work with an adult who cares about you.

I hope you will have fun doing this book, sharing problems and thoughts with others, and learning some important things to help you feel good about yourself.

There are times I feel happy and have fun.

(Draw some happy times.)

These are good times.

Other times I get in trouble and feel bad.

(Draw something you did that was wrong.)

Everyone makes mistakes. It is very important to learn from your mistakes.

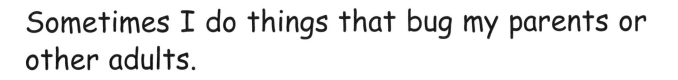

Sometimes I do things that bug my parents or other adults.

(Draw or make a list of these things.)

Most children have some problems with their behavior. Behavior is the way you act.

Sometimes I do something wrong to avoid being punished.

(Draw something you did that was wrong.)

Guilt that comes from not getting caught may feel worse than the punishment.

I can learn which behaviors cause problems.

(Check ✓ the behaviors you do too often and add a star ✱ to the ones you will try to change.)

Sometimes I:

_____ act bossy and tell others what to do.

_____ do not follow directions.

_____ will not share.

_____ do not follow rules.

_____ do not listen well.

_____ have a very messy room or desk area.

_____ cannot sit still very long.

_____ lie or cheat.

_____ hurt others.

_____ take other people's things.

_____ cannot get ready on time.

_____ do not finish chores or turn in school work on time.

Ask two adults to mark an ✘ after a behavior they would like to see you change. Talk about it together.

Feelings are something I feel in my body.

(Color the places you feel your feelings with the colors below.)

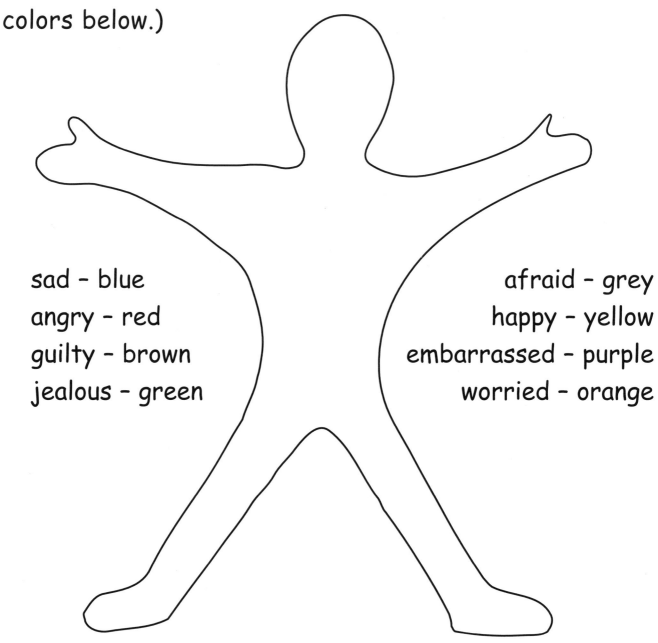

sad – blue
angry – red
guilty – brown
jealous – green

afraid – grey
happy – yellow
embarrassed – purple
worried – orange

It is important to know what you are feeling.
Your feelings affect your behavior.

Sometimes people put on a mask to hide feelings they don't want to show.

(Name and draw three feelings you sometimes hide.)

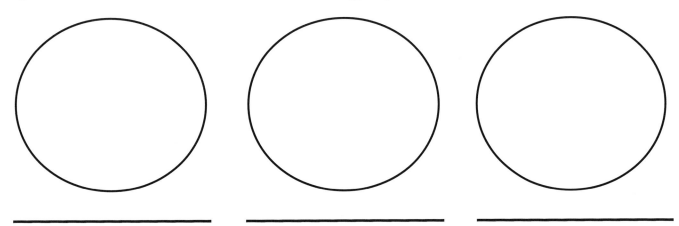

(Name and draw the "masks" you would use.)

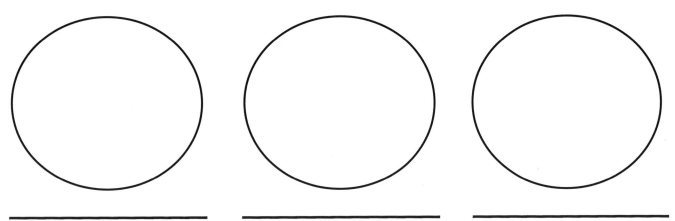

All feelings are OK. It is important to share your feelings with words. You can say, "I am feeling _____." You can only guess what others are feeling, unless they tell you.

Sometimes I feel sad.

(Draw a sad time.)

It is OK to cry to let your sadness out. It is not OK to use tears to get what you want. Words work better!

Sometimes I feel angry.

(Draw an angry time.)

Feeling angry is OK, but it is not OK to hurt people or things.

I can learn to let my anger out in ways that will not hurt people or things.

It is OK to:

1. Say "I am angry because _____."
2. Punch a pillow or a ball.
3. Yell into a pillow or in the shower.
4. Stomp my feet or clap my hands.
5. Write an angry letter and then tear it up.
6. Write in my journal.
7. Scribble on an old newspaper using many colors and feelings, then scrunch it into a ball and toss it against a bare wall.
8. Walk or run fast.

You are responsible for your own behavior. You can choose what to do with your anger.

Rude behavior makes other people feel uncomfortable.

(Draw some rude behavior.)

It is important to know how your actions affect others.

A consequence is the result of an action.

Keep off Thin Ice!

Someone didn't pay attention!

homework not done

(Draw or write the consequence.)

(Behavior)

(Consequence)

Adults use consequences to help children learn self-control.

There are consequences for my behavior at home.

(Draw or write some behaviors and their consequences.)

Good behavior   Consequence

Bad behavior   Consequence

It is important to learn from consequences.

Sometimes I can control my behavior to get a reward.

(Draw what you like to get for good behavior.)

Maybe the best reward is being able to like yourself ... and being liked by others!

Some behavior leads to punishment.

(Draw the ways you get punished. Then, circle the punishment that most helps you learn to control your behavior.)

Discipline is a way for adults to show they care and to help you learn self-control.

Sometimes I feel small and powerless.

(Draw a time when you felt powerless, then draw what you did to feel more powerful.)

Brain power can be stronger than muscle power. Always think before you act.

My feelings cannot make me do things I choose not to do. I can choose how to act.

(Think of an angry time. Then, think about your choices.)

Angry

Choices

Hit?   Ignore?

Yell?   Tell?

(Choose the best action and draw it.)

Feelings just happen, but you are not powerless over the way you act. Choose well.

Everyone must learn to think before they act.

(Draw someone bugging you.)

If I hit them instead of thinking, the consequence is:

_____

_____

_____

_____

_____   _____
(Think of a better choice.)   (Think of the consequence.)

You can control what happens to you!

Behavior Chart

(Make copies of this chart to use weekly. Give yourself a star ✱ each time you control your behavior.)

I will try to change these behaviors:

1. _____

2. _____

3. _____

Self-control is the ability to make good choices.
You can do it!

Behavior can be hard to control.

(Draw times that are difficult for you at home or at school.)

Everyone has some things they can learn easily and other things they have to work harder to learn.

These are the adults I live with:

Adults are responsible for children and need to make rules. Children must show respect and obey the rules.

My home has a few rules.

(Check ✓ the rules you have in your home, or add your own.)

_____ respect others
_____ no fighting or hitting
_____ no whining
_____ help each other
_____ pick up after yourself
_____ do your chores
_____ do your homework
_____ tell the truth
_____ practice good manners
_____ other:
_____ other:

Following the rules at home will help you follow the rules at school and the rules of the world.

Family members need to help each other with chores around the home.

(List some things you can do to be helpful and responsible.)

1. _____

2. _____

3. _____

4. _____

Decide when you will do each chore. Do your chores without being reminded.

You are needed. You are capable. You can help!

Chores Chart

(Copy and use weekly.)

My chores are easy to forget. Keeping a weekly chart and a regular schedule will help me develop good habits.

chore	Su.	M.	T.	W.	Th.	F.	Sa.
extra work							

When chores are well done, they may be rewarded. But in many homes, only extra work is rewarded.

Special privileges are the best rewards.

(Draw some special privileges you like to earn.)

(Draw something you are saving money for.)

A weekly allowance helps you develop good saving and spending habits.

My school has many rules. When I break the rules, I get in trouble.

(Check ✓ the behaviors that have caused you trouble.)

_____ talking too much

_____ bothering classmates

_____ not doing homework

_____ interrupting the teacher

_____ hurting others

_____ not listening

_____ turning work in late

_____ losing things

_____ acting restless

_____ laughing at others

_____ not telling the truth

_____ other:

_____ other:

Good behavior leads to better grades.

When I grow up, I would like to be a
_____.

(Draw a picture of yourself doing the kind of work you would like to do.)

Sometimes school may seem hard or boring, but school helps you learn to do what you want to do when you get older.

I can change my behavior to become a better friend.

(Star ✱ the things you do. Check ✓ those you want to learn to do.)

A good friend:

_____ treats others the way they want to be treated.

_____ tells the truth.

_____ helps others.

_____ acts kind and friendly toward everyone.

_____ doesn't blame others.

_____ asks for help when help is needed.

_____ shares and takes turns.

_____ follows the rules.

_____ asks for permission.

_____ respects self and others.

_____ smiles at me.

Good behavior leads to making and keeping good friends!

Some things are very hard for me to do, but I don't stop trying.

(Draw something hard to do that you are trying to learn.)

You can ask for help and you can keep trying to be the best you can be!

I am learning and I am trying. I will do my best to earn this reward ...

Signed _____